Come Fly with Me

And 21 Other Songs Recorded by Dean Martin, Ella Fitzgerald, Frank Sinatra, Sammy Davis, Jr., Sarah Vaughan, and Tony Bennett

CONTENTS

ISBN 1-57560-586-4

Visit our website at www.cherrylane.com

Come Fly with Me

Crooning the Cahn Classics

by David Simons

Though the years following World War II were a time of peace and prosperity, they marked the beginning of the end of big-band jazz, an American musical institution for nearly two decades. From out of the ashes of the decaying swing orchestras came a new epoch in American popular music, one that celebrated the artistry of the solo song stylist. With recording technology on the rise and television providing increased exposure, the 1950s quickly became the decade of the "crooner."

The shifting musical landscape would have a major impact on the career of songwriter Sammy Cahn, a proven lyricist with numerous hit tunes already to his credit. While still a teen in lower Manhattan, Cahn, a part-time violinist and full-time song plugger, scored his first major hit with Jimmie Lunceford's "Rhythm Is Our Business," a collaboration with piano-playing partner Saul Chaplin. By the 1930s, Cahn and Chaplin were on a roll, pouring out such top titles as "Until the Real Thing Comes Along" and the ever-popular "Bei Mir Bist Du Schoen," a breakthrough hit for the Andrews Sisters.

Cahn's next partner, Jule Styne, a gifted composer with a genius-like knack for melody, was an even better fit, and during the '40s and into the '50s, Cahn/Styne turned out some of the most covered songs in the country, including enduring classics "Saturday Night (Is the Loneliest Night of the Week)," the Christmas chestnut "Let It Snow! Let It Snow! Let It Snow!," and many more. Cahn's gift for crafting subtle yet sophisticated song lyrics guaranteed a non-stop crowd of crooning talent, with takers including Sammy Kaye, Bing Crosby, Doris Day, and Sarah Vaughan.

It was Cahn's connection to an up-and-coming Frank Sinatra that turned out to be the biggest bonus of all. Following his departure from the Tommy Dorsey Orchestra, the lanky young Sinatra delved into the Cahn songbook with gusto, covering "Things We Did Last Summer" and "Saturday Night (Is the Loneliest Night of the Week)," among others. When Sinatra signed on to do the 1945 film *Anchors Aweigh* with Gene Kelly, he made certain that Cahn was on hand to score the songs.

But by 1952, Sinatra's world was beginning to unravel, the result of a lost voice, lost recording contract, lost wife, and shattered spirit. Cahn, in the meantime, had parted company with Styne. When Cahn and Sinatra joined forces in the mid '50s, it began one of the greatest cavalcades of popular music the world has ever known.

Having parted company with Mitch Miller's Columbia Records in 1953, Sinatra got a new deal with Capitol, and, most of all, a new sound courtesy of crack arranger Nelson Riddle. For his part, Cahn got himself yet another winning cohort—composer Jimmy Van Heusen—and in 1955 handed Sinatra "(Love Is) The Tender Trap," the first in a series of stellar collaborations. From 1955 through 1962, Sinatra repeatedly mined the Cahn/Van Heusen collection, applying his vocal stamp to the likes of "Love and Marriage," "Come Fly with Me," and 1957's massively popular "All the Way." In election year 1960, Sinatra even turned a re-worded "High Hopes" into a winning campaign theme song for John F. Kennedy. Over the course of his career, Sinatra would record more songs by Cahn than by any other lyricist.

Cahn's link to Sinatra would have a few significant side benefits as well. The Cahn/Van Heusen score for the 1960 film *Ocean's 11* gave rise to the inimitable group of crooner cut-ups known as the Rat Pack, the Las Vegas–based wrecking crew featuring Sinatra and pals Sammy Davis, Jr., Dean Martin, and Joey Bishop. From their perch atop the stage of the Sands Hotel (otherwise known as "The Summit"), Sinatra and crew spiced up the all-night charades by giving top billing to such Cahn entries as "Ain't That a Kick in the Head" and "My Kind of Town" (from 1964's celluloid adventure *Robin and the 7 Hoods*).

Though Cahn could have easily subsisted on a straight Sinatra diet, other notable artists continued to raid the Cahn song cache. Like soul mate Sinatra, singer Tony Bennett found his voice and reached a mass audience during the pop-vocal boom of the 1950s. The same year that Bennett hit a commercial high with 1962's Grammy-winning "I Left My Heart in San Francisco," he tackled the Cahn/Van Heusen gem "Call Me Irresponsible" with characteristic clarity.

Even as rock music threatened the livelihood of many a veteran crooner during the 1960s, Cahn continued to pump out the standards, writing the title song to the 1967 film *Thoroughly Modern Millie* and, a decade later, starring in his own one-man show, *Words and Music*.

In 1993 Cahn passed away at the age of 80. By the end of the decade, Sinatra, Fitzgerald, and nearly every other living link to the great American song era had also departed. Yet the tremendous body of work they left behind will remain a part of the world's musical fabric for years to come. As Cahn himself once proclaimed, "The popular song is America's greatest ambassador."

Call Me Irresponsible

from the Paramount Picture PAPA'S DELICATE CONDITION

Words by Sammy Cahn

Music by James Van Heusen

Seems I'm al - ways mak - ing res - o - lu - tions, _____ like ev - 'ry night for me is New Year's Eve. _____ Things they chis - el on those in - sti - tu - tions, _____

the loft - y thoughts I nev - er quite a - chieve.

Each time I'm tak - ing bows 'cause ev - 'ry - thing went well,

things go a - wry, and there am I say - ing I meant well.

Slowly, with a steady rhythm

Call me ir - re - spon - si - ble,

Ain't That a Kick in the Head?

Lyric by Sammy Cahn

Music by James Van Heusen

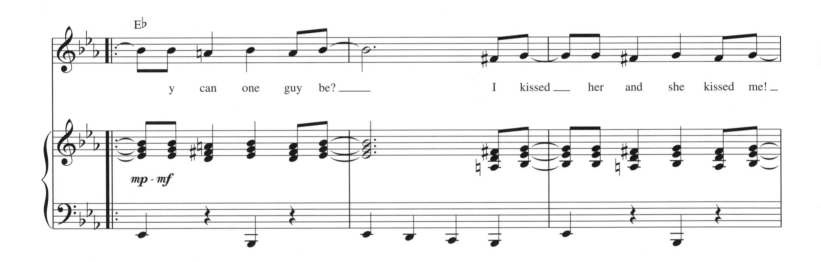

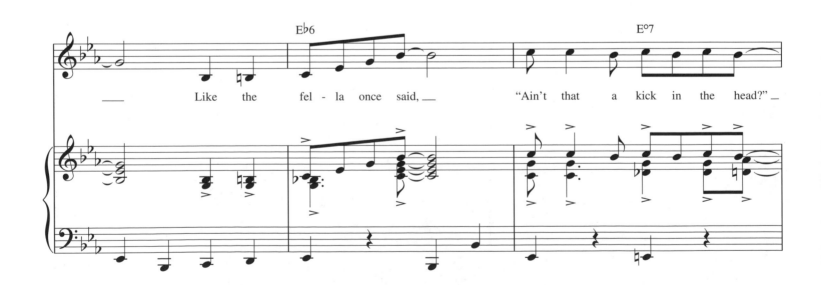

The room ____ was com-plete-ly black; ____ I hugged ____ her and she hugged back! ____ Like the sail-or said, quote, ____ "Ain't that a hole in the boat?" ____ My head keeps spin-ning, ____ I go to sleep and keep

11

All the Way

Lyric by Sammy Cahn

Music by James Van Heusen

Come Blow Your Horn

Lyric by Sammy Cahn

Music by James Van Heusen

Moderate beat

Make like a Mis - ter Milque - toast and you'll get shut ___ out, ___
Make like a Mis - ter Mum - bles and you're a ze - ro, ___

___ make like a Mis - ter Meek ___ and you'll get cut ___ out.
___ make like a Mis - ter Big, ___ they dig a he - ro.

Make like a lit - tle lamb ___ and wham! you're shorn; ___
You've got to sound your "A" ___ the day you're born; ___

Come Fly with Me

Words by Sammy Cahn

Music by James Van Heusen

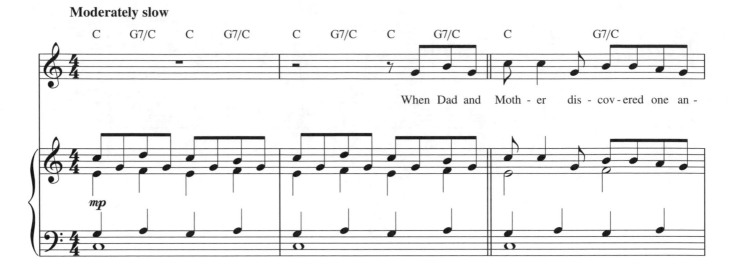

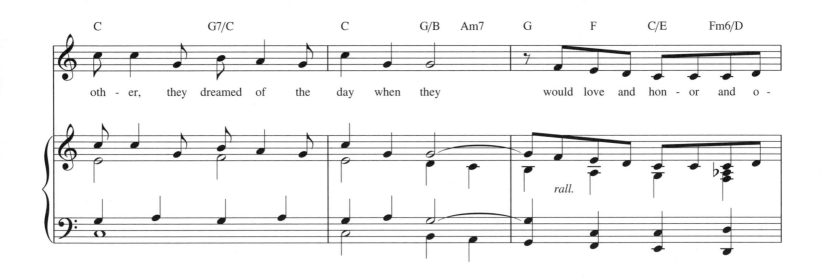

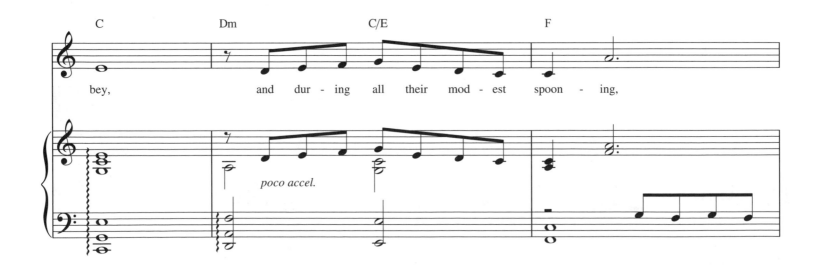

they'd blush and speak of hon-ey-moon-ing. And if your mem-o-ry re-

calls, they spoke of Ni-ag-'ra Falls. _____ But to-

day, my dar-ling, to-day, when you meet the one you love, you

a tempo

poco rit.

Moderately, with a strong beat (♩♩ = ⌐3¬ ♩ ♪)

say: _____ Come fly with me! ___ Let's fly! ___

mp - mf

star - ry - eyed. ___ Once I get you up there, ___ I'll be hold - ing

you so near; ___ you may hear ___

an - gels cheer 'cause ___ we're to - geth - er. Weath - er - wise, ___ it's such ___

a love - ly day! ___ Just

say the words __ and we'll beat the birds __ down to Ac - a - pul - co

Bay. It's per - fect for ___ a fly - ing hon - ey -

moon, they say. Come fly with me! __ Let's fly! ___ Let's fly ___ a -

1. way! _____

Come way! _____

mf

23

Day by Day

Theme from the Paramount Television Series DAY BY DAY

Words and Music by Sammy Cahn,
Axel Stordahl and Paul Weston

Ev'rybody Has the Right
to Be Wrong!

Words by Sammy Cahn

Music by James Van Heusen

As in vi-o-late, ___ as in ab-ro-gate, ___ as in lack-ing tact, ___ as in sor-did act, ___ as in thief or crook, ___ or sa-la-cious book, ___ it is wrong!

A word with tre-men-dous al-lure ___ be-cause it's pre-

Ev - 'ry - bod - y has the right ___ to be wrong ___ at least once! Ev - 'ry - bod - y has the right ___ to be dunce - like ___ once - like. ___ Not be - ing too smart is no dis - grace; ___ what sets ___ you a -

both _____ get a - long;   all it takes is   sim - ply say - ing you're

wrong _____ when you're wrong,   and ev - 'ry - bod - y   has the right _ to be

wrong.   it can be a   real de - light _ to be,

and I'd fight, fight   for the right _ to be   wrong,   at least   once!

Five Minutes More

Lyric by Sammy Cahn

Music by Jule Styne

High Hopes

Words by Sammy Cahn

Music by James Van Heusen

'stead of let - tin' go, just re - mem - ber that ant.
'stead of feel - in' sad, just re - mem - ber that ram.
they'll be burst - ing soon, they're just bound _ to go, "Pop!"

(Oops! There goes an a -
(Oops! There goes a
(Oops! There goes an -

Oops! There goes an - oth - er rub - ber tree plant.
Oops! There goes a bil - lion kil - o - watt dam.
Oops! There goes an - oth - er prob - lem, ker - plop!

oth - er rub - ber tree plant.)
bil - lion kil - o - watt dam.)
oth - er prob - lem, ker - plop!)

Oops! There goes an - oth - er rub - ber tree
Oops! There goes a bil - lion kil - o - watt
Oops! There goes an - oth - er prob - lem, ker -

plant.
dam.

plop!

Ker - plop!

Guess I'll Hang My Tears Out to Dry

Words by Sammy Cahn

Music by Jule Styne

I'm just as blue as the sky. ___ Since love is gone, ___ can't pull my-self to-geth-er. Guess I'll hang my tears out to dry. ___

Friends ask me out, ___ I tell them I'm bus-y; must get a new al-i-bi. ___

I stay at home ___ and ask my-self, "Where is { he?" } { she?" }

The Last Dance

Words by Sammy Cahn

Music by James Van Heusen

Love and Marriage

Words by Sammy Cahn

Music by James Van Heusen

Love and mar-riage, love and mar-riage go to-geth-er like a horse and car-riage. This I tell ya, broth-er, ya can't have one with-out the oth-er. Love and mar-riage, love and mar-riage,

My Kind of Town
(Chicago Is)

Words by Sammy Cahn

Music by James Van Heusen

all the things Chi - ca - go is to me. Gee! It's

Moderately

my kind of town. Chi - ca - go is

my kind of town. Chi - ca - go is

my kind of peo - ple, too, _____

my kind of razz - ma - tazz, _____

kind of town! _____

This is the Wrig - ley

Build - ing, Chi - ca - go is the Wind - y

Cit - y, Chi - ca - go is the Un - ion

(Love Is) The Tender Trap

Words by Sammy Cahn

Music by James Van Heusen

Pocketful of Miracles

Words by Sammy Cahn

Music by James Van Heusen

The Second Time Around

Lyric by Sammy Cahn

Music by James Van Heusen

say what led us to this mir - a - cle we
found? There are those who'll bet _____ love comes but once, and yet, _____
_____ I'm oh so glad we met the sec - ond time a -
round. _____ Love is round. _____

65

Saturday Night
(Is the Loneliest Night of the Week)

Words by Sammy Cahn

Music by Jule Styne

Rhythmically, not too fast

Sat - ur - day night ___ is the lone - li - est night ___ in the week ___

___ 'cause that's the night that my sweet - ie and I ___

___ used to dance ___ cheek to cheek. ___ I don't mind

Sun - day night at all ___ 'cause that's the night friends come to call, ___

Teach Me Tonight

Words by Sammy Cahn

Music by Gene DePaul

Did you say, "I've got a lot to learn?" ___ Well, don't think I'm try - ing not to learn. Since this is the per - fect spot to learn, teach me to - night. Start - ing with the "A, B,

Thoroughly Modern Millie

Words by Sammy Cahn

Music by James Van Heusen

think is chic, u - nique, and quite a - do - ra - ble, _____

they think is odd and Sod - om and Go -

Jazzy, rhythmic

mor - rah - ble! But the fact is: Ev - 'ry - thing to -
Ev - 'ry - thing to -

day is thor - ough - ly mod - ern. _____ (Check your per - son - al - i - ty.)
day is thor - ough - ly mod - ern. _____ (Bands are get - ting jazz - i - er.)

The Things We Did Last Summer

Words by Sammy Cahn

Music by Jule Styne

You're My Girl

Words by Sammy Cahn

Music by Jule Styne

they were wish - ing me well. They called me a luck - y
(you)

guy, and I could - n't hide ___ a feel - ing of pride. ___ You're
(I'm

my girl, ___ I've cho - sen you ___
your girl,) ___

___ to be mine ___ my whole life

Time After Time

from the Metro-Goldwyn-Mayer Picture IT HAPPENED IN BROOKLYN

Words by Sammy Cahn

Music by Jule Styne

Lyrics:
What good are words I say to you? They can't con- vey to you what's in my heart. If you could hear in- stead the things I've